LOST
IN
RETURNING
BACK TO THE
ORIGINAL
MESSAGE OF
JESUS

TRANSL

CHRISTIAN SANTIAGO

Copyright © 2019 Christian P. Santiago

Lost In Translation: Returning Back to the Original Message of Jesus

Cover Creation: Christian Santiago

ISBN: 978-1-7334030-0-9

Scripture quotations are from the ESV® Bible (The Holy Bible, English Standard Version®), copyright © 2001 by Crossway Bibles, a publishing ministry of Good News Publishers. Used by permission. All rights reserved.

All rights reserved. No portion of this book may be reproduced in any form without permission from the author, except as permitted by U.S. copyright law. For permissions contact via email: cs@christansantiago.space

The scanning, uploading, and distribution of this book via the Internet or via any other means without the permission of the author is illegal and punishable by law. Please purchase electronic editions and do not participate in or encourage electronic piracy of copyrightable materials. Your support of the author's right is appreciated.

Dedication

To my brother, Q. You epitomize what it means to hear the Father's voice and obey. You bring Heaven to Earth wherever you go.

What's Inside

Introduction   7

Section 1: Why did Jesus really come?

1. Establishing a religion?   17

Dealing with the idea that Jesus came to establish a new religion in Christianity. Religion v. Kingdom.

2. Getting us to Heaven from Earth?   31

Looking into the popular ideology that Jesus was focused on getting us to Heaven. Heaven from Earth v. Heaven to Earth.

3. Making us better?   49

Confronting the belief of a powerless Christ. Better v. New.

Section 2: Now what?

4. Be a Citizen, Not a Christian   71

We are not from here. We are from another place. What does that truly entail and how should we operate?

5. Embrace the Ambassador Within   95

The power of a position in the Kingdom that is overlooked. When understood, it produces power and provision.

6. Live as Sons and Daughters of the King 119
Embracing our role as a member of the Royal Family of Heaven. Squashing the poverty mentality.

Conclusion 141
Wrapping it all up.

Appendix: Prayer of Royalty 145
Acknowledgments 149
About the Author 151

Introduction

Communication is hard. It is not something that should be taken lightly, as it can often make or break the fabric of society. What do I mean by that?

In every level of our culture, whether the arena is politics, church, music, etc., the leading figures are people. What these leading figures do is lead other people, some do it by the thousands, others by the millions. How they lead them is through clear communication.

If the avenue of their message is a written policy, music video, or sermon, communication is used at a level of precision that is well-thought out, rehearsed, and delivered.

If they get the delivery of their messages wrong, masses of people are affected, families are not the same, and society as a whole cannot move forward towards the goodness of God. Communication matters.

If you don't believe me, ask yourself this question: Have you ever communicated a message of romantic interest to someone, but they interpreted a message of friendship? What about the other way around where you communicated a message of friendship, but they interpreted a message of romantic interest?

As humorous as these questions are, I ask you because I'm sure you have felt what it feels like to get your message lost in translation. Like you, I have experienced the same thing with my wife.

Lost In Translation

I met my wife, Chantal, on a mission trip in the Dominican Republic. We met halfway through our one-week trip during dinner simply because people from my team wanted to connect with "the other team from Australia".

Luckily for me, there was one remaining seat at the table, and it was next to Chantal.

The conversations and ministry time together that followed afterward captivated my attention towards the potential of who this Australian, powerhouse woman could be in my life.

During our free day the day after we met, we were walking together just discussing the dreams and plans we felt like God had for us individually. I was deep in thought when she abruptly changed the topic of conversation.

"So I want you to know that people keep coming up to me and asking if something is going on between us, but I told them that nothing is wrong with friends getting to know each other. I mean, that's all this is – *friends* getting to know each other, right?"

After springing that question, she stopped speaking, stood silent, and stared at me with those gorgeous, blue eyes waiting to see what my response would be. After experiencing a silence that felt like an eternity – mainly due to feeling caught off-guard – I responded, "Yes, that is *exactly* what we are – just friends getting to know each other."

And with that, I felt like the possibility of us riding off into the sunset with Mariah Carey's "We Belong Together" playing in the background was being placed into a coffin and lowered into the ground. It's a good thing I serve the God of second chances.

Even though God turned it all around and we both left the Dominican Republic with peace in our hearts about where our relationship was heading, I still think back to how uncomfortable it felt to have my message get lost in translation.

It was not easy to live in that tension because being lost in translation can cause the message to be misinterpreted, mishandled, or misrepresented.

I wonder if Jesus feels the same way. I wonder if His mission, message, and focus when He walked among us have been lost in translation. I wonder if it has been so lost in translation that His mission, message, and focus for us who call upon His name have misinterpreted, mishandled, or misrepresented Him to the world.

The effects of being lost in translation have been so severe that many people have walked away from the faith or have lost hope in the power of the Church. We have relegated the move of God to decades past and to the First Century Church that we cannot believe for a fresh wave of His Spirit in our personal and global world today. We have to believe again.

Returning Back

How do we get out from being lost in translation? How can we reclaim the impact on the world we were supposed to have as a Church?

How can we get back to waking up every day with excitement for the endless possibilities of what God wants to do and the ways He is going to show up?

We do this by returning back and recovering the original mission, message, and focus Jesus was entrusted with while being on Earth. The only way forward is if we turn back. We must look back with openness if we are going to move forward with clarity. Our perspective must shift if His power is to be shown.

As we journey together into rediscovering the original intent of the heart of Jesus, I want to encourage you to embrace and wrestle with what is contained in the following pages. They may hold truths you have never heard of, carry viewpoints you disagree with, and incorporate outlooks that bring the freedom you were intended to have when God sent His Son to save you.

Regardless of what our journey together consists of, I want to encourage you to ask yourself these tough questions in the presence of God. It is in the wrestling of tough questions and intense doubt that we encounter liberating answers and steadfast faith.

There are two main sections in this book. The first section is titled, "Why did Jesus really come?", which is all about tackling three big misconceptions we hold about the mission, message, and focus of Jesus during His ministry. These three misconceptions about His purpose are establishing a religion, getting us to Heaven from Earth, and making us better.

The second section is titled, "Now what?", which is about taking up our responsibility and embracing who Jesus really wanted us to be all along. It is about choosing to say yes to being a Citizen, not a Christian.

We will then talk in-depth about the power the role of being an Ambassador of Heaven plays in your life, and finally, how learning to fully accept our identity as a royal son and daughter of God Almighty will cause us to walk in authority we never had before.

My hope and prayer for you on this journey are ones of freedom and power. I pray that at the end of this book, you would walk in the security of who you were meant to be, and you would see God move tangibly in your life in a fresh way.

I pray you would move forward no longer carrying the burdens of your past and your soul would finally receive the rest it has been crying out for.

Now without further ado, let's look at the mission, message, and focus of Jesus in a new way, because if we don't, our world will get worse, our families won't change, and our lives won't be fulfilled. After all, no one enjoys the effects of being lost in translation.

Section 1

Why Did Jesus Really Come?

Everyone has their opinions on why Jesus came to Earth. Some say to get us to Heaven, others say to show us how to live.

These assumptions aren't far off, but they do not encapsulate the entire truth. Let's discover it from Jesus Himself.

1

Establishing A Religion?

Launching the modern religion of Christianity did not encapsulate the purpose of Jesus. He sought to establish something far greater.

Have you ever wondered what it takes to be a "good Christian"? Is it having perfect church attendance? It is knowing all of the popular Bible stories from David slaying Goliath to Peter walking on water? It is praying three times a day while fasting once a quarter? I only ask these questions because the answer during our modern times seems so elusive. The definition behind being a Christian has changed immensely over the years that we have now equated the term to someone who doesn't miss a Sunday gathering, helps with the church outreach twice a year, and is a nice person.

It seems as though being a Christian now has to do with participating in religious practices rather than participating in God's presence. We have a lot of churchgoers, but so few Christ followers.

Maybe this is because we have lost sight of what Jesus sought to establish while He walked this Earth. We have identified His mission as seeking to establish a new religion, Christianity. We could not be farther from the truth.

Setting The Scene

If we are going to understand what Jesus sought to establish, we need to understand who He is. For us to better recognize His identity and mission, answer this: Who is Jesus most like? A President, The Pope, or Caesar?

If you guessed The Pope, you guessed incorrectly. If you guessed a President, wrong again. The identity with which Jesus connects most to is Caesar. Why?

It is because they are both kings. Being a king from the beginning and until the end of time, establishing a religion was the furthest thing from our Lord's mind. Kings, unlike Presidents or Popes, aren't focused on popularity or piety, they are focused on conquest.

But many of us today, and the people of His time, seemed to miss it completely. Maybe this is because of the intricate details and world events of the time He stepped into.

When Jesus chose to put on flesh and step into the world as one of us, He came during the Roman Empire. This is significant for several reasons. First, the Romans were governing over the people of Israel, as well as conquering other nations.

What made the Romans unique in how the effects of their conquests took place included the use of colonization, which is the act of establishing control and authority of the conquered people by infusing it with their culture, laws, and officials.

The Babylonians nor the Persians utilized the strategy of colonization in the manner the Romans did when their empires took center stage in the world.

Second, there was a 400-year silence of God's voice among the people. No prophet stood up in the synagogues proclaiming the revelation of God's will after being overcome by the Holy Spirit. Generations would live and die never hearing, seeing, or feeling the power of the Creator of the Heavens and Earth. The time frame between Malachi and Matthew may last one second for you and me, but it lasted four centuries for Israel. If we can't survive in our world without knowing God is with us for a day, how much harder was it for them?

Lastly, what made the entrance of Jesus during the Roman Empire remarkable had to do with them allowing Israel to continue their religious practices. They still permitted them to attend every synagogue meeting, even as they began to infuse that area with Roman culture. Even though Israel no longer had their territory, they still had their religion.

Ultimately, Jesus was stepping into a world where the Roman Empire heavily utilized colonization, the people of Israel have not heard from God for 400 years, and religion took center stage. Each one of these factors are substantially weighty when we consider the identity of Jesus and what He purposed to establish. These factors directly affected his interactions with every man and woman of His day – particularly, the "good Christians".

"Good Christians"

As Jesus began His earthly ministry at the age of thirty years old, He came into frequent conflict with a group called the Pharisees. Now before you go and write them off as the normal bad guys of the New Testament, let's take a look at who they are with a fresh set of eyes.

The Pharisees were a part of the religious "elites" of their day. They were known for completing all of the acts written in the Law perfectly, never missing a synagogue gathering, memorizing the entire Old Testament, fasting regularly, praying multiple times a day, and giving large amounts of money as offerings.

If we looked at them with contemporary eyes, these would be the people who never missed a church service, whether it occurred on Sunday or Wednesday. They would instantly recall any Bible verse to mind when asked, fasted multiple times a year, not just on a 21-day Fast to start the new year. They prayed three times a day and did not allow anything to get in the way of that and gave more than the prescribed ten-percent tithe.

In modern terms, the Pharisees were the ideal picture of a "good Christian". In fact, I would dare to say these people were better Christians than you and I. They prayed, fasted, and gave more than you and I combined. We were not even close to their dedication, and yet Jesus consistently proclaimed a message they always seemed to miss. The train Jesus conducted was moving forward and they were not on it.

If the Pharisees were the picture-perfect model for modern Christianity, what did they miss that we often miss today? Let's look no further than the rebuke Jesus gave them.

> "But woe to you, scribes and Pharisees, hypocrites!
> For you shut the *kingdom of heaven* in people's faces.
> For you neither enter yourselves nor allow those who
> would enter to go in." (Matthew 23:13)

The Pharisees did not miss out on a new religion, for they were the elites of their sect. What they missed was a Kingdom. Jesus rebuked them because they possessed membership in their local synagogue, but did not possess citizenship in the home country of Heaven.

This exclusion of the Pharisees through the rhetoric of Jesus reveals a starting fact many of us in contemporary Christianity has misunderstood – He did not come to establish a new religion in Christianity, He came to establish a Kingdom.

All our Lord preached about during His time on Earth could be summed up in the Kingdom of God coming to meet us. His focus and purpose did not include our 21st Century Christianity. He spent His days among us bringing His timeless, powerful, and spiritual Kingdom into the physical world. He accepted nothing less.

If there is tension present to believing this, consider His first words after being fully commissioned for ministry through the baptism of John and temptation of Satan,

> "Now after John was arrested, Jesus came into Galilee, proclaiming the gospel of God, and saying, 'The time is fulfilled, and *the kingdom of God* is at hand; repent and believe in the gospel.'" (Mark 1:14-15)

He charged His disciples with preaching about the gospel of the Kingdom when He sent them out.

> "And he called the twelve together and gave them power and authority over all demons and to cure diseases, and he sent them out to proclaim *the kingdom of God* and to heal…And they departed and went through the villages, preaching *the gospel* and healing everywhere." (Luke 9:1-2,6)

Jesus even continued preaching about the Kingdom of God after His resurrection!

> "He presented himself alive to them after his suffering by many proofs, appearing to them during forty days and speaking about *the kingdom of God*." (Acts 1:3)

Even the disciples knew Jesus sought to establish a kingdom. They just thought it was the kingdom of Israel instead of the Kingdom of Heaven!

> "So when they had come together, they asked him, 'Lord, will you at this time restore *the kingdom to Israel*?'" (Acts 1:6)

If the focus and purpose of Jesus mainly consisted of establishing a new religion that emphasized only the cross, why did He preach about the Kingdom of God after He rose from the dead and defeated Hell, death, and Satan?

Now before you begin thinking that I do not cherish the work of the cross for us and label me a heretic as you close this book, hear my heart. The cross is absolutely essential for everything. We cannot enter into the Kingdom of God without it. We are unable to gain citizenship into the Kingdom of Heaven if we are not born into it and we are only "born again" (John 3) through Calvary.

But how do the themes of atonement and sin that are prevalent in the sacrifice of Jesus fit into the gospel of the Kingdom? When Adam chose to sin and disobey God's command in Genesis, he acted against a King – and not just any king, but a perfect, holy, and righteous King.

As with all acts of rebellion, our King had to punish it fully. When we rebel against a king, we cannot expect anything less than death. The cross is where the wrath of God is satisfied.

What I am sharing throughout these pages are the answers to what many Christians ask after they say 'yes' to Jesus: "I'm saved. Now what?"

Kingdom vs. Religion

Religion kills. The Kingdom gives life. Religion adds regulations and rules. The Kingdom grants freedom from performance. Religion answers the question of, "I'm saved. Now what?" with insincere and repetitive piety. The Kingdom answers it with passionate purpose.

Jesus did not come to bring us a life of regimented practices that do not involve genuine participation from the heart. He did not desire for us to say 'yes' to Him only for our lives as Christians to be defined by our church attendance, Bible knowledge, and nice attitudes.

Even the term 'Christian' has lost its meaning from when it first described the disciples in the Book of Acts.

> "And the hand of the Lord was with them, and a great number who believed turned to the Lord... So Barnabas went to Tarsus to look for Saul, and when he had found him, he brought him to Antioch. For a whole year they met with the church and taught a great many people. And in Antioch the disciples were first called *Christians*." (Acts 11:21,25-26)

The disciples were first called 'Christians' in Antioch by others who observed a group of people that preached boldly despite widespread persecution, performed miracles, experienced exponential growth through salvation, and impacted every city they resided in. Doesn't this sound a lot like the ministry of Jesus?

The people of their time did not have any other terms to describe this group of people, except that which they already witnessed with the man from Nazareth. They bestowed on them a term that is defined as, "little anointed ones", no doubt signifying the similarities they carried in comparison to the original Anointed One.

This begs another question: does this sound anything like the current state of the modern church? Are miracles, boldness despite persecution, exponential growth, and transformation of the cities we are settled in describe us now?

If you are honestly observing, as I am, you would agree that this description does not accurately paint the picture of our churches, or even more personally, our own lives. This should not only confuse us but create a hunger deep inside of us to rediscover the gospel of the Kingdom.

We have done religion, ritual-based Christianity for too long and reaped the consequences for it. Families are being torn apart, nations are deteriorating rapidly, and people are leaving the church by the generations with the thought, "Been there, done that. It wasn't for me." When the true gospel is preached – one which is founded on the Kingdom of God – then lives will be changed, cities restored, and nations saved.

We will be aligned with the same gospel Jesus and His disciples proclaimed all throughout Israel, and we will finally see the return of our King.

> "And this *gospel of the kingdom* will be proclaimed throughout the whole world as a testimony to all nations, and *then* the end will come." (Matthew 24:14)

Jesus did not come from Heaven and put on our flesh to establish a religion. He came to establish a Kingdom. He did not come to make us subject to guilt and shame if we do not pray every day or fast twice a year. He came to bring a Kingdom to Earth that would make us sons and daughters of the King without us needing to prove ourselves.

Make no mistake – Jesus did not come to make us Christians, He came to make us Citizens. It's time we started embracing that fact. Reject Religion. Accept the Kingdom. Change the world.

> "I assign to you, as my Father assigned to me, *a kingdom*" (Luke 22:29)

2

Getting Us To Heaven From Earth?

>  *Jesus was less focused on getting us to Heaven and more focused on getting Heaven in us. This was not a rescue mission, but more of an invasion.*

Being born and raised in Florida, there are three constants: humidity, mosquitos, and hurricanes. Some may argue for alligators to be thrown in there, but most of that is dependent on where in Florida you live. No matter where you reside in the Sunshine State, you can expect to sweat, get bit at night, and have to wait in line for an hour for the next shipment of water to arrive because of a natural disaster nearly every summer.

With Chantal being from Australia, she did not know what to expect when her first major hurricane knocked on our door. She had mixed emotions – both of excitement and nervousness. I personally felt indifferent towards the possibility of the hurricane, since this would have been the eighth I experienced in my lifetime.

This particular hurricane began as a Category 4, but lessened to such a degree when it made landfall that Chantal's response to all of it became, "That's it?" Even though her first hurricane experience did not reveal the true destructive nature of what this storm could become (as I've witnessed in my childhood), one thing did occur that took both of us by surprise.

It was 3 o'clock in the morning and my immediate family were all sleeping soundly together when suddenly we heard a blaring alarm. I instinctively woke up with the immediate thought, *Fire! We are all going to burn!* I proceeded to shake everyone until they awoke so we could complete evacuation protocols. Dealing with fire on its own can be tough but when you add a hurricane to the mix at the same time, you have a recipe for disaster.

Within minutes, everyone in our apartment building began to check their homes for a fire, and declared, "All clear!" from their balconies. After hearing the "All clear!" from every neighbor, we soon realized the alarm was tripped by a lizard that got caught inside one of the consoles and fried as a result. Poor lizard.

As we returned inside and tried to sink back into the deep slumber we were shaken out of, I could not help but ask myself why I felt an immense amount of fear upon hearing the fire alarms. After a couple of minutes, I soon realized the reason for my fear is because I did not want to burn.

Negative v. Positive Motivation

When I first think about why I started following Jesus, all I could think about was the desire to acquire fire insurance. I wanted some kind of insurance to protect me from experiencing the flames of Hell. I desperately desired to avoid the bad place and enter the good place. Needless to say, I had negative motivation for following Jesus.

Negative motivation can only take you so far in your journey with Christ. If the sole reason why you want to eat healthy and exercise is because you do not like how you look in the mirror, there's most likely going to come a point where you are going to look one last time after trying so hard and seeing no results only to quit.

Negative motivation may get your journey started, but it's not strong enough to sustain your journey. I've never seen shame produce complete transformation in my life and I have a feeling the same is for you. Positive motivation, on the other hand, works much better than negative motivation. It is powered by a passionate 'why'.

If the reason for eating clean and challenging yourself through physical exercise is to be functionally capable to play with your grandchildren when you get older, then your strength and vision for what you are doing will sustain you to keep going, even if you've had a tough week. It will cause you to rise early and work late. It will inject passion inside your heart to run after something worthwhile and give more today than you gave yesterday. Your grandkids will be grateful later that you thought of them now.

When it comes to your walk with Christ, ask yourself: is it based on a negative or positive motivation? Have you chosen to follow Him because you need fire insurance or because of something much more? The desire to escape Hell is not inherently bad – especially since Hell is real and no one deserves to experience complete separation from God – but it is not enough. We need a greater 'why'.

Religion v. Kingdom

As Jesus walked this Earth and lived out His mission, He attacked religion and established His Kingdom. One of the very things Jesus sought to destroy in religion is the belief of holding out for Heaven.

It seems as though the primary reason contemporary Christianity proclaims Jesus came to humanity was to get us to Heaven from Earth. That the main purpose of the ministry of Christ is to secure us a spot in the good place and help us avoid the punishment of the bad place.

It says we must be content in our anger, happy with our poverty, and satisfied living in our depravity here on Earth as long as we prayed that one special prayer. This could not be further from the truth of His message. My hope for you is that after this chapter, God would plant a powerful positive motivation in your heart as to why you have given Him your life. Discovering His original intent sure changed my life.

Heaven To Earth

When it comes to the subject of Heaven, the main focus on the heart of our King can be found in the first few lines of the often-quoted section we call The Lord's Prayer.

> "Pray then like this:
> 'Our Father in heaven, hallowed be your name. Your kingdom come, your will be done, *on earth as it is in heaven.*'" (Mathew 6:9-10)

It seems rather interesting Jesus did not focus too much on getting us to Heaven. When teaching on prayer, He did not pray, "God, help them to hold out until I come back!" or "God, teach them how to live with their dysfunctions until they get to Heaven."

He wasn't focused on a rescue mission; it was about an invasion. His exact words had nothing to do with getting us to Heaven from Earth, and all about bringing Heaven *to* Earth. What's noteworthy about Jesus praying this particular line in verse ten connects perfectly with how the Roman Empire functioned.

Our Lord intentionally stepped into this time period so He could speak specific truths in this manner and people would understand. All He would need to do is point to the current climate of their world for them to fully comprehend the implications of His words.

When Jesus said, "on earth as it is in heaven", the people knew exactly what He was implying. This phrase reflects a strategy the Romans used during their worldwide conquest.

During their time, whenever the Romans would conquer other kingdoms, they would establish colonies. Within the colonies they established, they would infuse the conquered culture with their own.

From the architecture to the arts, they desired for the colony to possess the same atmosphere and feeling as Rome itself. The Romans would make sure the culture and environment reflected the exact culture and environment of their homeland.

They sought to replicate in the colony the experience and feeling of the palace, especially whenever Caesar traveled throughout the Empire. Their objective was for Caesar to have the same experience in the outwards lands as he had at home.

The intention of Earth was to be a colony of the Kingdom of Heaven. When God placed Adam in the Garden and gave him a mandate to rule, it was meant for him and his descendants to rule as He did.

Since we are made in His image, we are called to govern in such a way that all of creation would not see us – they would see God. This is why the Scriptures tell us that all of creation are waiting for the revealing of the sons and daughter of Almighty God (Romans 8:19).

Adam had been given an assignment to make the culture and environment of Earth to reflect the culture and environment of Heaven. When he and Eve sinned in the Garden, he gave up that right and lost his authority. This is why the second Adam, Jesus Christ, came to restore the authority which was lost, and reinstate Man's ability to make Earth reflect the very likeness of Heaven.

In essence, Jesus prayed the line, "on earth as it is in heaven", so we would take the mission of bringing Heaven to Earth and not rest until we see His Kingdom of peace, joy, healing, strength, wholeness, power, and love actualize in the world around us.

Just as the Romans sought to transform colonies to reflect the palace when Caesar would come, so we must seek to transform the colony of Earth to reflect our homeland of Heaven before our King Jesus returns. We must work tirelessly, fight ferociously, and sacrifice willingly to see our world changed to look like the Kingdom of our God. We must be willing to do whatever is necessary to revolutionize culture of Earth to match the culture of Heaven.

Why are we called to help the needs of the homeless? Because in Heaven, there are no homeless people. Why should we seek to bring healing and relief to those who struggle with mental illness? Because in Heaven, there are no struggles with mental illness. Why should we seek to reconcile racial tensions? Because in Heaven, everyone is highly esteemed.

The church needs to get this message. We must not quit and choose to relegate our time on Earth discussing issues that do not matter, being content with feeling good but not really changing anything, and preaching a message about holding out for Heaven.

We were never called to wait to get up to Heaven; we were called to fight to bring Heaven down. We were commissioned to make the spiritual Kingdom of Heaven manifest in the physical realm of Earth.

We must take up the call of the King to spread His influence everywhere we go with our actions. We must say 'yes' to spreading the gospel of the Kingdom of God with our words. His Kingdom is here and the realities of all it entails wants to invade the colony of Earth.

As Christ's ambassadors, we must represent Heaven on every matter and create the same environment as our homeland. We need to live in such a way that Heaven breaks out in all we do.

Heaven In Me

Many of us genuinely want Heaven to invade Earth. We truly believe with our whole hearts God still does miracles today with the intention of saving lives and transforming the culture. The only issue is before Heaven can break out in the world around us, it must break out in the world inside us. Before Heaven can invade my job, it must invade my home. Before Heaven can invade my city, it must invade my marriage. Before Heaven can invade my region, it must invade my heart.

I have followed Jesus faithfully for a decade and this truth has eluded my life for most of it. I have witnessed God performed miraculous signs and do things I could not explain, but those moments were rare, to say the least, all because I did not believe I could experience Heaven right now.

I believed the lie religion told me in that I had to wait until I died to experience its goodness. This made my depression somewhat bearable, my family's poverty explainable, and my apathy for the life of Christ understandable.

Everything changed for me once I discovered the gospel of the Kingdom Jesus constantly preached. Once I realized I did not need to wait to die to experience Heaven's favor, provision, healing, joy, power, and peace *right now*, I pressed forward enjoying all of the goodness Jesus offers as my King.

So, I urge you, my brother and sister, embrace this message. Embrace the proclamation and commission on your life to bring Heaven to Earth.

Embrace the power God has placed inside of you to radically shift the atmosphere of every room you walk into because you said 'yes' to Him. Embrace the responsibility to make Earth reflect the very likeness of Heaven.

When you do that, don't be surprised when God begins to make Heaven invade your life and impassions your heart with a mission that will never grow cold, even to the day you see Him face-to-face.

As you begin to live the way you were meant to live, you will become a catalyst to transforming the politics, media, fashion, medicine, education, arts, family, and social media of our culture into the image and likeness of Heaven. You will see Earth alter completely to prepare for the return of its King. You will become whom Jesus foretold His disciples would develop into when the Holy Spirit comes upon them in power – witnesses to the ends of the Earth.

A Final Encouragement

As we journey deeper asking our Father for His will be done on Earth as it is in Heaven, I want to encourage you about something specific. It is the key to encountering Heaven in your home, heart, and health. This key is fixed on Jesus being a King and His mission focused on establishing His Kingdom, not a religion.

God is serious about His glory. He will not share it with anyone else (Is. 42:8) and is always seeking to expand it on Earth.

During the times where ancient kingdoms waged war against one another, many of the reasons for these campaigns originated with the king's desire for more land, people, resources, and influence. In simplest terms, the greater influence a king possessed, the greater their glory. The growth of their glory happened to be directly proportional to the growth of their control and influence.

The key to experiencing Heaven invade every facet of your personal life is to completely abandon building your kingdom and give your life to expanding the Kingdom of God.

It means that when you wake up in the morning, your first thought shouldn't be, *How am I going to pay my bills?* It should be, *How can I spread the influence of my King today?*

Once your mindset shifts to this kind of thinking, do not be surprised if the Holy Spirit leads you to a coffee shop you would not have otherwise visited to speak to a person you never met to give them a personal encouragement they have never received before.

It will be through that personal encouragement where they surrender their lives to King Jesus, His influence in the world grows, and His glory over the Earth expands. You will have aided in spreading His reign over the Earth because you surrendered to living with a Kingdom mindset. When you focus on the Kingdom of our Father, He will meet and exceed your needs for financial breakthrough, marital reconciliation, and supernatural healing.

It is only natural for an earthly king to reward those who have contributed to the growth of their influence and glory, especially during times of intense warfare. If an earthly king blesses subjects who extend their kingdom, how much more will our King bless His sons and daughters when they do the same, especially in times of intense spiritual warfare?

When your focus is on extending His reign in other people's lives rather than trying to make it out on your own, then God will supply your every need in the most miraculous ways. When you seek to bring Heaven to Earth, you begin to notice God's hand and favor over your life greater than ever.

Now, as you go forward pursuing a cause or mission that will bring the Kingdom of God down so that Earth reflects Heaven when Jesus returns – whether it is racial reconciliation or providing clean water – keep your eyes fixed on the King, because when you focus on the King, the King will surely focus on you.

> "But seek first *the kingdom of God* and his righteousness, and all these things will be added to you." (Mathew 6:33)

3

Making Us Better?

> *The power of Jesus is not limited to making us better. He has the power to make us new. Instant transformation is not for the select few.*

Have you ever experienced the phenomena known as buyer's remorse? Some of our minds immediately traveled to last year's Black Friday sale, or Boxing Day in Australia, where we bought hundreds of dollars worth of material things we stopped using three months later. While not everyone can identify with buyer's remorse, I do believe there is another remorse we all can identify with.

I want to coin the phrase "committer's remorse" with you. Ultimately, committer's remorse is when you make a commitment to someone, something, or somewhere and feel the same regret in the pit of your stomach you would after making a fool-hearty purchase.

My committer's remorse occurred after the second week of starting a new job. This feeling of loss and regret began when I heard the words from my supervisor, "You're not getting paid today. You'll get paid next week. Payroll is behind."

Those words sank deep in my gut and – in an instant – I developed emotions of disgust for both my job and myself for continuing to work there. I possessed a keen intuition this problem might occur before I took the job, but I needed it because Chantal and I were in our first year of marriage.

I also happened to be the only one bringing in any type of income because she could not work until her immigration process was complete. We needed every penny at this point.

Maybe your committer's remorse is nowhere near as bad as mine or maybe yours was much tougher. Regardless of where you find yourself in the spectrum, one thing we do have in common – our emotions of remorse can be traced back to the sentiment of feeling *stuck*.

When that sinking feeling occurs in our gut, it's mainly because we feel helpless, powerless, and hopeless to change anything. This affects us and causes a victim mentality to develop within us while forcing us to live in a physical, emotional, and spiritual rut.

Sadly, once we encounter the depth of this rut, some of us resolve to live there for the rest of our lives. Things should not be this way.

It is just plain wrong when the children of God are held captive and settle for lesser lives because of these ruts. Jesus meant much more for our lives. He meant much more for *you*.

He wants to get you out of the rut you're living in right now. He wants to pick you up out of the mud and place your feet on dry ground (Ps. 40:2). The only way He will do it, though, is if you do not settle for just "better" and say 'yes' to "new".

Better v. New

It took three months for my job situation to change. I refused to wait around for my current job to get better and instead sought a new one. Even if my current job improved, or got "better", it does not mean it would be beneficial, since I would need to properly define what "better" actually means.

If my employer chose to pay me five days late instead of eight days, by its proper definition, my job situation got "better". If they chose to train me once a week instead of telling me to get the job done without any assistance, my job got "better". I knew deep in my heart that God did not want "better" for me – He wanted "new."

Many of us have unconsciously accepted the belief that when Jesus came to Earth, His ministry was all about saving us and making us "better". When He filled us with the Holy Spirit, His ministry of "better" included struggling with anxiety for four days of the week rather than the usual six days. Or dealing with shame from the past only in the mornings as opposed to the flashbacks occurring both in the morning and at night.

You may already feel secure in your heart that Jesus did not come to settle for making us "better". You might even think that every Christian knows that Jesus came to make us "new", but do we *actually* believe that? We may profess this with our mouths, but do our underlying beliefs and lives reflect these truths?

If you want to know whether these are truths you live rather than truths you profess, ask yourself these questions:

- Do you actually believe Jesus can and will heal you completely from your mental illness ***today*** or do you believe He will help you cope with it for ***the rest of your life***?

- Do you actually believe Jesus *completely* wiped away and forgotten your past or do you believe Jesus uses your past as reference points to help you as your shame goes away *little-by-little*?

- Do you actually believe Jesus completely changed your identity into royalty *now* or do you believe Jesus will make you royalty when you get to **Heaven**?

- Do you actually believe Jesus can miraculously transform your situation *today* or do you believe Jesus will do it *eventually*?

Each of these questions has been specially crafted to excavate the presuppositions hidden within our hearts about the mission of Jesus, as it pertains to this essential topic. The crux of the matter is many Christians have settled for "better" rather than expecting the "new".

We have given up on the possibility of receiving the fullness of Christ here on Earth that the world has taken notice and turned to *their* methods of "better". They have taken cues from the Church and do not see Jesus as Someone who can instantly and powerfully transform their lives. They see Him as Someone who was a good man that can make them better human beings when all the while they are longing for the "new".

We must recapture the heart of Jesus in this matter if we are going to be a lighthouse to a world headed for the perilous rocks of destruction and eternal separation.

New Creation

In the Kingdom of God, people do not enter in with their old identity – they receive a new one. They are "born again" (John 3) and given a new name before Heaven, for several reasons.

One reason, in particular, has to do with our rebellion and treason. When we sinned against our King, we were choosing to rebel from His reign. However, endless amounts of love for us filled our King's heart and He chose to die in our place.

In order for His justice to be satisfied and the sin of treason properly punished, He must become us and our sin, due to the fact that in a kingdom, the exact rebels must be punished, and not anyone else. This is why Christ became sin for us (2 Cor. 5:21) and we have been crucified with Christ (Gal. 2:20).

In the aftermath of Calvary, our sins of treason were forgiven by the King, and our old identities were killed. Since our father was no longer the devil (1 John 3:7-10), we became orphans. As a result, the King chose to adopt us and call us His sons and daughters.

He performed a new birth in our hearts and were given the Holy Spirit, so we would carry ourselves in the same Spirit our new family lives. As Jesus established His Kingdom on Earth, He desired us to be "born again", because His intention was for us to become "new creations" (2 Cor. 5:17).

Newborn babies are the perfect example of a "new creation" we can clearly see in our world. Some of the qualities they exhibit in our world are ones we are called to exhibit in this Kingdom we have been granted citizenship in.

Traits At A Glance

- ⇒ Don't have a past
- ⇒ Don't deal with shame
- ⇒ Completely dependent on their caretakers
- ⇒ Take cues on how to operate in this world by their parents as they grow

All of these traits listed easily point to one effect the Kingdom of God creates – making us "new", not "better". Jesus did not call us to operate in His Kingdom by bringing the rules, regulations, habits, mindsets, and lifestyle choices from our old life, even if we tweaked them to make them "better".

We needed to become blank canvases for Him to properly infuse us with the rules, regulations, habits, mindsets, lifestyle choices, blessings, and authority of Heaven.

No person can expect to live correctly in one place operating under the assumptions of another. Our hearts needed to be wiped completely clean of the baggage we carried in order to take on the burden He desires for us to carry (Matt. 11:28-30).

For our baggage to be completely clear, He chose to wipe away and forget our jaded past once we fully accept His sacrifice and repent ("turn away") of our old lives.

After embracing the finished work of Calvary with our whole hearts, He then bestows on us a new identity. It is one that does not have a past, is not riddled with shame, places us in the palace as royalty, and calls us to dive deeper into the heart of our Father, the King.

Our lifelong pursuit no longer becomes one of us trying to escape what is behind us, as it no longer exists in God's mind (Is. 43:25), but one of focusing on what is in front of us (Phil. 3:13-15) – which is to establish the Kingdom of our God on this colony we call Earth.

We have been called by God through Jesus Christ to become sons and daughters of Almighty God, ambassadors of His Kingdom, and citizens of Heaven. Where you and I are truly from, our homeland of Heaven, people do not struggle with their anxiety, because they live in perfect peace. Where we are from, people do not struggle with worry, because they are wholly dependent on the King's ability to provide, as He has never let His people down.

We must learn to accept that Jesus did not come to make us "better", He came to make us "new". He did not come to make us "better" Christians, but to make us a "new" creation.

> "So if the Son sets you free, you will be free *indeed*."
> (John 8:36)

Out With The Old, In With The New

As we have journeyed together to discover the call to be "new" rather than "better", some of you have been wondering how to actually live in that reality.

We desire the *what*, but do not have any prescribed steps for the *how*. It is equivalent to a doctor giving a diagnosis, painting the picture of what life would look like once you're healed, and then sending you home without prescribing a remedy for the solution. The steps to take towards the penultimate life of the "new" Jesus promises us can be found in Mark 9:15-24. There are three simple, yet profound actions we must implement to embody the identity we have been entrusted with and take advantage of the life we have been given.

As the scene opens in verse 15, Jesus is coming down from a mountain with His three closest disciples – Peter, James, and John – and stumbles upon a commotion. The other nine disciples attempted to cast out a demonic spirit in a boy and were largely unsuccessful.

Noticing the miracle worker from Nazareth shows up, the boy's father then pleads for Jesus to step in. He agrees and as He steps closer to the boy, the evil spirit convulses Him terribly. This prompts a side conversation with the father about the boy's childhood, and then He finally commands the spirit to leave.

Let's jump in on how the final exchange goes as a whole, and then highlight specific portions of this passage that point to the three steps to actualizing the fullness of our "new" life.

> "And when Jesus saw that a crowd came running together, he rebuked the unclean spirit, saying to it, 'You mute and deaf spirit, I command you, come out of him and never enter him again.' And after crying out and convulsing him terribly, it came out, and the boy was like a corpse, so that most of them said, 'He is dead.' But Jesus took him by the hand and lifted him up, and he arose." (Mark 9:25-27)

1. **Come to Jesus believing for a *permanent* change.**

As Jesus follows through with bringing freedom to this boy's life from the grip of the enemy, He delivers a proclamation that reinforces His mission of "new", which is available for everyone who believes.

> "And when Jesus saw that a crowd came running together, he rebuked the unclean spirit, saying to it, 'You mute and deaf spirit, I command you, come out of him and *never enter him again.*'" (Mark 9:25)

Did you notice Jesus did not say, "leave him alone for six years" or "stop convulsing him on Monday's, Thursday's, and Saturday's"? He commanded the spirit to *never* return. Jesus knew He possessed full authority to offer absolute freedom and there was nothing Satan could do about it.

Jesus also knew the only thing that counts as authentic freedom is freedom that *lasts.* If freedom from the afflictions which bind us is only temporary, then it is not powerful.

If the freedom we receive from Christ still lands us in slavery occasionally, then it is no better than Moses leading the Israelites to the Red Sea only for God not to deliver them, forcing them to return to a life of chains.

But Jesus does not offer a counterfeit type of freedom to us. Because King Jesus genuinely sets people free who are under the rule and captivity of Satan, those who come to Him must desire and believe the freedom they will experience is permanent. They must not only believe Jesus can heal them permanently but wants to heal them completely.

They must throw aside the notion society brings that complete and utter healing in an instant is not for everyone that comes to Jesus, but only for the select few. Our Savior does not offer a different kind of salvation to multiple people. Everyone has the same opportunity to be healed permanently, completely, and instantly. If Jesus offered a different kind of salvation for multiple people, then it would be contrary to His nature and character.

If what society – and some church circles – proclaims is true about this kind of freedom being for the select few, then the King we serve is a prejudicial one, who only regards certain men and women as deserving of an instant transformation, while everyone else is relegated to the struggles of slow, monotonous change and the life of "better".

Because we know God is not a respecter of persons (Acts 10:34-35) and gives equal access of His power to anyone with a willing heart without regard to race, gender, socioeconomic status, upbringing, personality, etc., His salvation for permanent transformation is for you. All you must do is *take Him at His word.*

2. *Expect* a struggle.

Once Jesus commands the evil spirit to leave the boy, something interesting happens. The boy does not instantaneously walk away completely free. The evil spirit does not immediately leave. In fact, things get worse, terribly worse.

> "And after crying out and convulsing him *terribly*, it came out, and the boy was like a corpse, so that most of them said, 'He is dead.'" (Mark 9:26)

The first time the boy convulses in front of Jesus, Mark is clear it was not a welcoming sight for onlookers (v. 20). The second time it occurs, it is subsequent to the command of Jesus to leave and never come back.

Mark notes the second convulsion was demonstrably worse than the first, as he supplements the word "terribly" to signify the difference. What does this tell us about living in the "new" Jesus came to bring? The devil is not going down without a fight. We should not be surprised when things get worse, even for a moment or season.

In order for a breakthrough to manifest in our lives, we must break through something. Resistance always precedes a breakthrough. Things get tough because the enemy is losing his grip on your life and wants to maintain control.

It is equivalent to me trying to take a toy out of a child's hands and they react by choosing to grip the toy even tighter. Or when God tries to cause a relationship or an employment season to end in our lives, but we battle Him for greater control. When things are being taken away from us, the natural reaction is to hold on tighter and force the struggle to be harder than it needs to be.

This is exactly what happens when Jesus rebukes the evil spirit. Satan did not want to give up control of the boy, or of you, but he has to surrender no matter what when dealing with the King.

Expect a struggle after accepting the permanent transformation Jesus brings. Make the choice to put on your armor for battle and persevere for the long haul. The call to "new" over "better" is not a pretty one, just as labor is not a sight to behold. But never forget that both the battle and labor pains yield the fruit of a new creation.

3. Move forward *fully* relying on Jesus.

After Jesus commanded the evil spirit to leave and it convulsed terribly, the boy finally experienced freedom from Heaven. What transpired afterward leads us to our final step.

> "But Jesus took him by the hand and *lifted him up*, and he arose." (Mark 9:27)

In a world which advocates self-reliance and independence, this verse flies in the face of everything many of us in the West, and other regions, have been taught. After the evil spirit left the boy for good, he seemed dead. The battle for his soul took its toll and he laid limp. When Jesus touched him, he came to life and encountered the power our Savior carries to lift us up.

On the contrary, what the boy did *not* do is something we must ponder internally. As Jesus began the act of lifting him off the ground to his feet, he did not push away the Messiah to lift himself up.

He did not tell Jesus, "Thank You for saving me, but I have it from here. I can stand up on my own two feet." He did not reject the help offered to him in order to display the personal strength and independence he possessed.

What does this tell us? If we are truly going to live in the Kingdom of God and experience the fullness of the "new" our King gives us, we must entirely cast off the mindsets of independence and self-reliance. In the Kingdom of Heaven, the sons and daughters of the King are designed to be like little children who fully rely on their King and Father for everything.

If we are genuine followers of Christ, there should be no such thing as self-reliance in our hearts. Instead, complete reliance and dependence on the Father to work everything out in our favor should exist. This does not mean we live a life of laziness or lack initiative while fostering an attitude of entitlement. It just means our personal strength, wisdom, resources, and intellect are not the sources of our hope and reliance.

When citizens of a kingdom are choosing not to rely on their king, they are declaring their own independence. When we declare our own independence, then *we* will be required to keep all of the doors opened in our lives. Whoever opens the door must keep it open.

This is why it is vital to embrace our citizenship over accepting the religious identity of a modern-day Christian. Citizens rely on their King, while Christians attempt to make things happen in their lives and then proclaim, "It wasn't God's will" when it does not end favorably.

So there you have it, the three things you must do to enjoy the "new" Jesus offers over the "better" modern religion offers. You no longer have to settle for living in a rut and can finally be free from the shame of your past, the insecurities and struggles of your present, and the worries of your future.

Now that we have clarified the mission, message, and focus of Jesus on Earth with establishing a Kingdom, bringing Heaven to Earth, and making us new, let's move forward together to understand how to practically live in the Kingdom of God.

Section 2

Now What?

It is not enough to know something if we don't do something about it. Faith without works is dead. If we do not know how to bring Heaven to Earth or live out our Citizenship, then we are wasting our time together.

Let's venture further and learn how we can complete our journey of bringing the Kingdom of God to Earth.

4

Be a Citizen, Not a Christian

There are many Christians in church, but very few Citizens of the Kingdom. It's about focusing on the Kingdom over just "doing church".

"I have a brain tumor."

Those words shocked me to my core as I heard them proceed out of Jean's mouth. I ran into him moments earlier on my university campus and asked him the usual question many of us default to, "How are you?" His response was unlike any other during that particular day. My conversation with him served as a friendly reminder to be ready in and out of season.

He began with telling me about the first seizure he ever experienced a few weeks prior and how this caused part of his face to go completely numb for a couple of hours. After the seizure and some medical attention, the doctors performed a CAT scan which ultimately revealed the brain tumor. Jean shared this entire story with me, including the part of him feeling the shock after receiving the results a day earlier.

"They're going to do surgery on my brain."

With those words to finalize the answer to my question, he stared at me with a look that communicated both a genuine worry and an earnest plea for me to do something. At that moment, I did what I knew to do – something I grew accustomed to doing, but now with a fresh perspective on who I was.

*　　　*　　　*　　　*　　　*

"The thief comes only to steal and kill and destroy. I came that they may have life and have it abundantly." (John 10:10)

The words in John 10 are ones you have probably heard quoted if you have been around church long enough. They would ring out almost weekly as I grew up in a pew. It is a vivid picture of the contrasting life Jesus and Satan offer us. There are two plans seeking to work in our lives – one that steals from us and one that gives to us.

Like many of us, I grew calloused to the heart behind the words of Jesus simply because the modern-day Christian life did not seem to offer this so-called abundant life. To me, it seemed as though it revealed to be the opposite. But this begs the question: if the life we experience does not line up with how Jesus proclaimed it would be, could it be attributed to us living the wrong way?

Christianity v. Citizenship

As previously discussed, to be defined as a "Good Christian", the modern definition of a Christian has changed dramatically over the centuries. What defined you as a Christian before doesn't today.

For one to be a "Good Christian", they must attend church more than once a month, be able to recall Bible stories like Noah's Ark or Peter walking on water, and be a relatively nice person who just bites their tongue in silence so they don't offend anyone.

Whether or not your Christian walk can be identified by this description, you possibly have experienced the emotional weight of being burned out by a cycle of practices that truly do not bring passion to your heart and purpose for your life, as I have. This is why new converts or many people I have grown up with inside the church have made the choice to walk away from it all.

The contemporary Church has answered the questions of, "I've said 'yes' to Jesus. Now what?" with a plethora of rituals and practices that are designed to bring us alive in His Kingdom, but have been reduced to a spiritual checklist that is completed to avoid the sentiments of guilt and shame. Striving to be a "good Christian" is no longer enough.

The striving to fit into this modern definition of Christianity has stripped the true Gospel of its power in our lives. We're burned out, apathetic, and consistently sense the "been-there-done-that" emotions. Something must change in our lives for us to reclaim the life Jesus promised us in John 10:10. It's a good thing He gave us the Kingdom.

Being a Kingdom Citizen changes everything. It lights a fire in your belly, gives you excitement for your future, and brings you closer to the heart of God than ever before. The antidote to the effects of our contemporary Christianity are the powerful effects of our Heavenly Citizenship. After all, the gospel of the Kingdom is what Jesus preached.

What Does Citizenship Entail?

When I initially discovered the concept and message of the Kingdom of God, I did not understand it. I encountered more confusion than clarity, especially as I ventured deeper into the topic of our Heavenly Citizenship.

I asked a two-fold question you may be asking yourself:

What does it truly mean and what effects will it have on my life?

Since we have been able to perform a deep-dive into the Kingdom of God, let's talk about the intricate details of our Citizenship. Once you are able to grasp this for your personal and family life, it will transform your work and community life. Here's why – the power in who we are lies in where we're from. The power is in the passport sealed by the Holy Spirit through the application process of the blood of Christ approved by the courts of Heaven.

As a Citizen of the Kingdom of God, incredible rights and privileges have been bestowed upon you. To access them and live to the fullness of our original design, we must understand how citizenship works. What better picture to reflect our Heavenly Citizenship than looking at how our earthly citizenship works?

I am a citizen of the United States of America. This citizenship gives me specific rights, privileges, blessings, and responsibilities. I do not cease being an American Citizen when I am visiting another country. I am always a citizen of my home country unless I perform an act that would cause me to lose my citizenship (when you break the law you lose rights uniquely tied to your citizenship).

As we surrendered our lives to Jesus and were born again in the process, we gained a new citizenship – one that takes precedence over all other ones that may be in our possession. This does not negate our earthly citizenship rights, as it is possible to possess dual-citizenship.

One of the benefits of possessing citizenship rights to more than one country is the ability to lean on the citizenship that is more fruitful, especially during the event of the diminishing of a country's conditions. One can retreat to the more prosperous and stable country if they hold the rights to that country.

This is why I am seeking to earn my Australian Citizenship through my wife. It does not mean I do not believe in the future of the United States – it just means that if things go sour, I have another place to retreat to.

Our Citizenship with Heaven works the same way. The Earth is wasting away little by little, day after day. One day it will be completely gone. Those who have surrendered their lives to the King will be granted access to the Kingdom of Heaven because of their Holy Spirit-sealed passport. Those who do not will be turned away at the gates, where there will be weeping and gnashing of teeth.

Being a Citizen of Heaven means you live by a different set of rules. It means that your day-to-day habits and circumstantial responses reflect your difference. It results in you standing out from the people in proximity due to your nature being different from theirs. When cultures from two contrasting countries collide, either confusion, conflict, or change occurs.

This reminds me of the first time my wife, who's Australian, met the 4-year old son of my senior pastor from Florida. He truly loved wooing people with his charm and playing silly practical jokes, as many kids under the age of ten enjoy doing.

After observing him play a few jokes on others, Chantal openly remarked, "Wow, he's such a ratbag." Clearly stunned, I asked her plainly, "Did you just call our pastor's son a ratbag?" After noticing it came across as an insult, she quickly attempted to clear her name of all guilt, "It means mischievous where I'm from. It's a term of endearment to kids who use their cuteness to get away with things."

After this silly exchange of conflicting cultures, I soon realized how easy it would be to stand out in a place that is not our norm. It is the same with those who belong to the homeland of Heaven. You will be misunderstood, you will be labeled, you will be challenged. It is the reality of belonging to a Kingdom that is unseen to people who aren't a part of it.

Being a Citizen means you are defined by a country that is invisible but lasts forever. Being a contemporary Christian means your identity is mostly defined on what you do for two hours on one day of the week.

*   *   *   *   *

"Can I pray with you right now?"

Jean's eyes softened as I made this request, but also seemed uncomfortable about praying in the middle of the university courtyard with scores of people passing by. Honestly, I was a bit uncomfortable too, but I chose to offer immediate prayer because I had been previously guilty of giving the usual, "I'll keep you in prayer", without actually following through with it.

I grew to become angry of this because the revelation of being a part of a Kingdom movement had begun to perform a deep work in my heart. I desired the real thing and the real Jesus – not some Jesus that is regulated to my Sunday's and leaves me to figure life out on my own throughout the week.

Jean needed the real thing and an authentic touch from Jesus. He needed the true power of God to heal him and perform a supernatural miracle that only comes from Heaven.

My expectations for a miracle were not very high at that moment, but I inwardly knew the King wanted to heal him more than my faith to believe.

"Sure, prayer would be great."

Sensing the uncertainty in his voice, I smiled and assured him that I would be there for him regardless of what happens next. I laid hands on his shoulders, and not on his head to avoid drawing unnecessary attention to ourselves.

During the prayer, something noteworthy occurred. A sense of boldness began to arise within me. I no longer offered the fear-filled prayer of, "If it's Your will, please heal him." I began declaring healing and wholeness over his body in the name of Jesus – as if I knew I held authority over this sickness.

After what felt like an eternity – which really turned out to be six minutes – we finished praying. Needless to say, we could not verify if he had been healed instantly (due to his condition being hidden away in his brain) and yet the look on Jean's eyes told the whole story.

> "Thank you. I really needed that. I was honestly scared and freaking out, but I'm not anymore."

And with that final statement, we promised to stay in touch after his surgery and parted ways. Even though his medical procedure was in a week, I wouldn't see Jean for another three months.

*   *   *   *   *

There are a multiplicity of ways we can venture deep into the Kingdom of God and how we as Citizens operate within this powerful Kingdom. The Kingdom Gospel is so multi-faceted and sophisticated to such a degree that I can speak about it for hours.

It is truly life-changing and powerful. Sometimes Chantal tells me to ask people if they have time for a lion's share of information after they inquire about the Kingdom of God.

I don't want it to be overwhelming for anyone – as we have already covered a lot – because my desire is for everyone who reads this book to be able to implement changes in their lives, habits, and thinking on Monday. It is for this reason that we will speak about just three major ways Citizens of the Kingdom of God operate. These are simple, but not easy, undertakings you can begin to integrate into your daily life and will produce radical transformation.

How to Live Like a Citizen

If you are able to grasp these three lifestyle shifts, you will see Heaven become active in your daily life. You will no longer characterize your life as mundane and ordinary and will instead define it as exciting and supernatural. The three ways Citizens of Heaven operate can be simply described as obeying the King, emulating Heaven, and pursuing the King's heart.

1. Obey the King.

In any kingdom, both earthly and Heavenly, the foundation it rests on is obedience to the king. It is the highest priority for every citizen. If disobedience is welcomed for one citizen, then that seed has the power to transform into a weed and spread to the rest of the kingdom. This small weed of disobedience can be the likely cause of a revolt.

As a Citizen of the Kingdom of God, obedience must be our highest priority. We cannot expect or even hope for the blessings of the King without fully obeying Him. This may be tough for us to comprehend because in our democratic society we are allowed to criticize our leaders, give our opinions, or refuse their command. In a kingdom, these acts might cost you your life.

Because obedience is greater in the Kingdom of God than acts like fasting or praying for hours (1 Sam. 15:22), we must cultivate it in our daily lives. Since Jesus is a King and not a President, Citizens must act immediately upon His request.

His identity as King is the reason why both partial obedience and delayed obedience is disobedience in His eyes. When a king makes any request, his citizens must carry it out immediately and to its fullest extent. If we are going to operate successfully in the Kingdom of God, there is an imminent need for us to put aside our democratic mindset. We must lay down our opinions and be willing to say 'yes' to His command, even if it does not make sense or people see us as crazy because of it (2 Cor. 5:13).

This does not mean we neglect to share our feelings with God, as He is a personal and loving King, but we must not interpret His kindness to hear our hearts with His acceptance of our disobedience. We cannot confuse His grace with allowance or license to sin. If we cannot obey, we cannot succeed.

2. Emulate Heaven.

I love going on international mission trips. It is incredible to see the power of God manifest in an environment that is foreign to me.

What's also great about these trips is how fast you are recognized as a visitor by the locals. It seems as though how we carry ourselves and how we look causes us to stick out in a crowd.

Citizens of the Kingdom are called to carry themselves in the same manner. We are born again into a new homeland, Heaven, and live in such a way that it communicates loudly our set-apartness, i.e. holiness. The way we handle adversity, praise, and circumstances shows the world that we are not from this world. Unfortunately, many of us aren't sure how to emulate Heaven simply because we haven't visited it yet. What we can rely on, however, are the laws Heaven is built on. If we infuse our lives with the power of the Word of God, we will know how we are supposed to operate here on Earth.

If we know our homeland is built on unlimited forgiveness after hearing about God's extravagant forgiveness for us (John 3:16), then we will not carry any offense in our hearts.

If we know the culture of Heaven is predicated on honoring people, even before they deserve it or if they have dirt in their lives (Matt. 13:44), then we will uplift and respect the people around us. In the Kingdom we're a part of, we live by laws that are unlike the ones of this world. Many of them are based on the condition of the heart, not the condition of our circumstances.

We forgive before the offenders apologize, honor before our bosses deserve it, and love before our inner circle reciprocates it back. All of the laws within the Kingdom are designed for bringing transformation wherever the Citizens accurately display the qualities of their King.

Living by the principle of emulating Heaven has provided open doors for greater forms of ministry, deeper reservoirs of wisdom, and a closeness with my wife I could not fabricate. When we now have our "heated" discussions, it dissolves much more quickly due to the realization that people do not tear each other down where we are from. We have made the radical decision not to live for Heaven, but to live *from* Heaven. You should, too.

3. Pursue the King's Heart.

In a kingdom, everything is about the king. The entire kingdom under his dominion rests on his name. If his name no longer holds power, his kingdom will soon crumble.

In the Kingdom of God, everything rests on the name of Jesus. Without Jesus our King, there would be no Kingdom. Without Him, there would be no Heaven. In His name, there is power, authority, and healing every Citizen has access to.

Unfortunately for many people who wear the name of Christ on them as a Christian, they do not live as though their entire life rests on the King. They say 'yes' to Him once a week and live in a self-reliant manner for the other six days. This may be how a Christian operates, but it is not how a Citizen operates.

A Citizen lives as though their life would fall apart if they weren't close to their King.

Since all of Heaven is founded on our King Jesus, their personal foundation would be destroyed if not for His presence. In order to remedy this bleak outcome, Citizens stay close to the heart of their King. They know that their life is nothing without the consistent closeness of Jesus, day-in and day-out.

It is in the daily closeness of Jesus where the blessings, rights, and privileges of Heaven draw near because wherever our King goes, He brings His Kingdom with Him. Our souls need to be close to Him to also be drawn away from our bent towards self-centeredness. We cannot hope to receive all that He has for us if we are only thinking of ourselves.

If we pass or fall away, the Kingdom of Heaven will still be there. If King Jesus does, however, there's no hope for anyone. Once we make our King the entire focus of our lives and His Kingdom the emphasis of every breath, we will receive the clarity, vision, healing, and power of Heaven. We will live supernatural lifestyles that were meant to characterize every follower of Jesus, not just the select few.

So choose today to obey the King, emulate Heaven, and pursue the King's heart. Trust me, you won't be disappointed with how your life is used for purposes greater than yourself.

*   *   *   *   *

"Hey Christian, did I ever tell you about my procedure?"

It was three months since I last interacted with Jean. It felt like an eternity from the previous time we spoke that I actually forgot what he was referring to.

"What procedure?"

Jean then kindly reminded me about the brain tumor the doctors discovered and how we prayed a week before the procedure was completed.

"How did it turn out? It seems like you're recovering well."

With my limited scientific and medical expertise, I would think surgery on the brain would take a long recovery period coupled with side effects on top of it all. What struck me as odd was the fact that Jean look exactly as he did three months prior.

> "That's the crazy thing, Christian. When the doctors opened up my head, they were confused. They did not find the tumor anywhere. It was completely gone. I never thought this would happen."

This left me speechless. I possessed the same level of faith Jean had. We both didn't think anything would happen. I knew I felt a greater sense of boldness and authority at the moment, but the result still brought shockwaves to my body.

All I could think about doing was giving him a tight hug and proceeding to yell loudly while jumping as if I lost all sense of my social surroundings. It was in the jumping and yelling of praising God for this miracle that I realized I no longer have to live a purposeless and boring Christianity.

I discovered that day what it meant to be a Citizen of Heaven and how this could translate into changing the world around me while cultivating the life Jesus promised inside of me.

I pray this day is the same for you. That you would embrace your Citizenship and reject the modern definition of what it means to be a Christ follower.

Be a Citizen, not a Christian.

5

Embrace the Ambassador Within

> *Being an Ambassador for the King is one of the most prominent positions in the Kingdom of God. It grants unparalleled provision and authority.*

"We may be short on money, but I feel like God wants us to buy their dinner."

Being well into the first year of our marriage, Chantal and I were like many couples in the beginning stages of their marriage – full of life and empty of money. Our situation happened to be unique from many others, as Chantal could not work for eight months due to completing all of the necessary steps for her immigration status to be changed.

During this season of fierce reliance on provision from Heaven, we learned that everything we owned (which was not much) belonged to God, including the little bit of money we possessed. He did not own a tenth of our money – all of it was His.

It was the sixth month of Chantal's work hiatus when she came to me about one of our close friends from church that was struggling to have food for dinner. We ourselves were struggling for money, but I knew God placed this generous desire to buy our friends dinner in my wife's tender and powerful heart.

> "Let's go for it. Call them and we'll come over to cook some steaks for them."

And with that, I knew this was going to be a leap of faith because all the margin in our budget for that month amounted to only $35. We were going to need a small financial miracle if a steak dinner for four people was going to equal or be less than that amount. In other words, we needed Jesus to multiply steaks for our sake just as He multiplied bread.

*   *   *   *   *

All of those who have accepted their place as Citizens in the Kingdom of Heaven carries a desire within themselves to bring Heaven down to Earth. We desire to see the supernatural financial breakthroughs, marital reconciliations, the salvation of loved ones, and miracles of healing take place in our world. Inside of our souls, there is a yearning to see the impossible come to pass.

I want you to know that this internal groaning is normal for those who call Heaven home. This groaning even occurs all throughout Creation (Rom. 8:19). These groanings may seem radical to the world and for those within the modern church, but this is the type of faith Jesus expected all of His disciples to display. It is only foreign to us because we have normalized an ordinary life for every believer.

Check out what Jesus actually says in Mark's version of the Great Commission and see for yourself if ordinary or supernatural is supposed to define our lives,

"And he said to them, 'Go into all the world and proclaim the gospel to the whole creation. Whoever believes and is baptized will be saved, but whoever does not believe will be condemned. And these signs will accompany those who believe: in my name they will *cast out demons*; they will speak in *new tongues*; they will pick up serpents with their hands; and if they drink any deadly poison, it will not hurt them; they will *lay their hands on the sick,* and they *will recover.*'" (Mark 16:15-18)

Jesus entrusted the mandate and mission to transform Earth to reflect Heaven to His people, you and me. But how do we do that? How can we bring Heaven to Earth? And if we are successful, what would it look like?

Bringing Heaven Down

Roughly around the 17th Century, Great Britain conquered the Bahamas and made it into a colony. They began to imitate how the Romans established colonies and began to infuse its politics, arts, and lifestyle into the tiny island. As decades began to pass, the locals adjusted. They started to sip on tea and speaking with an accent. This transfer of British politics, arts, and lifestyle is known as an infusion of culture.

As we are called to bring Heaven to Earth, our main role is to bring the culture of Heaven into existence. We are designed to force the unseen realities of the spiritual Kingdom of Heaven into the seen realities of the physical realm of Earth.

We are made to change Earth into such a place that everyone speaks with the language of faith and love, while not settling for anything less than what Heaven offers us. Everything we do and say must reflect the country we represent. In essence, to effectively bring Heaven down we must bring its *culture* down. And for us to do that, we must embrace our role as Ambassadors.

You Are So Much More

As Citizens of the Kingdom of Heaven, our identities are multi-faceted. We are not minimized to just one role. This may scare some because we have a plethora of responsibilities, but may energize others because great responsibility is attached to great power and influence. Spider-Man would agree ("With Great Power Comes Great Responsibility").

Knowing our multi-faceted identity created a lasting peace inside of me because I no longer need to be incarcerated by the label of "preacher", "pastor", or "author". I can be so much more.

You too no longer need to be limited by the labels of "teacher", "mother", or "doctor". You can now become the all-encompassing influencer of culture God destined you to become without any limitations provided by the labels you may have received in life.

Being a Citizen beckons us to be ambassadors, conquerors, kings and queens, servants, and other prestigious positions in the Kingdom. It is truly exciting to be alive and a part of the Kingdom. One of the key identities we have been entrusted to operate as is one of an ambassador. This role is one that is essential to gaining the keys of authority, protection, and provision.

Like some of you, I wrestled with why being an ambassador even mattered. I personally read several Bible verses about it but didn't really pay any attention to it. I did not see any value in the position.

That is, until the day I began to research what it actually entailed. It completely changed my mindset and I'm sure it can change yours. Let's dive right in.

Identity of an Ambassador

Simply put, an ambassador is an individual who is a representative of their home country in a foreign land. The land they live in is not their true home. Their loyalties lie with the country they represent and they seek to live in their assigned country with the highest standards of their true home.

Ambassadors are approved by the country leader after several background checks and high-intensity interviews. They are placed under a large amount of scrutiny before being given the green light.

After they are fully approved and placed in their assigned foreign country, they are given the full authority to speak on behalf of their homeland, as long as they stay in constant communication with their leader to maintain the position of their country.

They do not communicate anything other than the policies, constitution, and opinions of their home country, not even their personal thoughts or desires.

In ancient times, ambassadors not only communicated the exact words of the king, but they also expressed the exact *tone* of the king. The tone of your voice is just as important as the content of your words. In short, ambassadors are entrusted with high amounts of responsibilities, but there are high amounts of blessings given to them, too.

*   *   *   *   *

"Hey Christian, glad you and Chantal are coming over and bringing steaks. Can you also buy zucchini and asparagus as well?"

As I am walking into the grocery store after work to buy the steaks for dinner, this text reaches my phone. At first glance, feelings of anger began to flood my body and thoughts of rages filled my mind.

How could they ask for more?

> *Don't they see we are doing this for them?*
> *We only have $35 for steaks, zucchini, AND asparagus?*

In an instant, I heard a whisper in my heart from God, *"Christian, don't worry. $35 will be enough. Trust Me, it's My money anyways."* And with that, I filled the cart with steaks, zucchini, and asparagus.

> "Hey Christian, would you also be able to buy the New York Strip steaks? Those are our favorite. Thank you, brother."

By this point, I was internally fuming. When things get tough financially, my first instinct isn't to pray, it's to calculate. And that's exactly what I did.

I added up all of the items, including the more expensive New York Strip steaks and the sales tax, and realized I would be three dollars short. This meant we needed to use money from savings to meet the need. And again, I heard the whisper of God, *"My son, don't worry. $35 will be enough. Trust Me, it's My money anyways."*

The first time I heard God whisper, I trusted. The second time, I calculated. Upon hearing His second whisper, I continued the necessary transfers from our savings for use. I did not exactly emulate the definition of a cheerful giver.

Emotions of betrayal for obeying and anger for being generous resided within my heart in that very moment, but it would all eventually subside as God completely shocked me ten minutes later.

*   *   *   *   *

By now, you are probably wondering what the point is to be an ambassador. We know it is a biblical concept, which is expressed by the Apostle Paul (2 Cor. 5:20), but the real question we have yet to answer is: Why should *you* embrace this position in the Kingdom? Why does it seem to hold such importance in every Citizen's life when welcomed fully? Maybe sharing about the blessings of an ambassador might motivate and explain to you why it is valuable..

Blessings of an Ambassador

There are two primary blessings ambassadors carry that apply to those who hold the title – authority and provision. Being approved after the scrutiny and background checks mean the ambassador can be trusted with the authority of an entire nation.

When an ambassador is living in their assigned place, they possess the power of their entire government. Where an ambassador resides speaks further to the authority presented in their position.

As countries set up relations with one another, they establish embassies, which are places of sovereign soil that represent the full authority of the country the ambassador speaks for.

In an embassy of the United States in France, the establishment of the government building is the exact representation of the United States itself. This means if an individual takes one step inside of that embassy, they are on U.S. soil, even if they are not physically there.

As ambassadors of Heaven, wherever we place our feet, God has established His embassy there. In our homes, jobs, neighborhoods, cities, and families, the installation of Heaven has occurred. The sovereign soil of Heaven is settled everywhere we go. God has given us the authority of a full country to bring about change as we are planted on Earth.

Just as ambassadors have access to the authority of Heaven even as they are assigned to the foreign country of Earth, they also have access to the blessings and benefits of Heaven while being on Earth. They are not only provided with full authority to get the job done, but they are also granted admission to divine and unlimited resources.

As ambassadors seek to fulfill the assigned term (i.e. our life span on Earth) in their assigned country, they are furnished with the supplies of their home country for them to be successful in all of their endeavors. They are not subject to the financial systems of the country they reside in but are subject to the finances of their home.

If their assigned country goes bankrupt, they are unaffected and untouched. Ambassadors do not have to worry unless the economy of where they are from goes downhill. Brothers and sisters, we no longer have to be subject to living a life of worry for our King will not allow His representatives and children to go hungry or suffer lack (Ps. 37:25).

We are reliant on the economy of Heaven, which has no limits and never suffers under the effects of famine, droughts, and market crashes. He will always provide for us, even when everything around us is crumbling.

We can smile, keep our peace, and retain our joy in the Lord because of our trust in our King and His Kingdom. The heart of our Father to provide and take care of us under extreme circumstances is unquantifiable. His affection towards us is unrestricted, therefore His resources towards us are unlimited. He has not failed His children in the past, and He will not begin doing it today. He is a good Father who never leaves His children unprepared to accomplish His will.

Becoming an Ambassador

The identity of an ambassador contains more power than many of us truly realize. Like you, my mind expanded in awe of God due to the revelation of this position of high esteem.

I originally held a presupposition of its inferior nature because of my lack of understanding. Now my eyes are wide open, and I hope yours are, too.

Unfortunately, this newfound understanding of this role is not enough to change our lives. If we are to receive the blessings and authority of an ambassador, we must operate as one. We cannot obtain the fullness of God if we are unwilling to live under the fullness of His covering through daily surrender.

Now, there are four simple steps you can take to embrace your calling to be an ambassador of Christ. Consequently, these action steps require a renewing of our mindsets and heartsets. You must choose to "be" before you choose to "do."

1. Know your constitution.

The Kingdom of Heaven is predicated on the establishment of the laws of the King. Every square inch of Heaven is founded on every word that proceeds out of the mouth of God. The Creator's words are so powerful that even the physical realm of Earth depends on them (Heb. 11:3).

One of the main responsibilities ambassadors must carry is the ability to represent their country's stance on every matter. They cannot offer their personal stance or opinion if they are going to be a great ambassador. Highly-opinionated ambassadors do not last long, as do less-knowledgeable ones.

If an individual is going to function as a representative of their country, they must know every policy, amendment, law, and constitution of it. It is a necessity to be well-versed in every aspect of their government's position on specific matters. This is precisely why the people of God need to know Heaven's constitution, the Bible.

We must consume every facet of our Bible if we are going to accurately and successfully represent Jesus here on Earth as His body. We have many Christ followers who claim to live in the Kingdom of God but do not know what positions they should take.

If the Church did not change so much on their stances over the years on specific matters and only communicated what Heaven desires, maybe we would see more lives changed. But it is not too late to see change in our world. All we have to do is change ourselves. It must begin at the micro level (the individual believer) before it can affect the macro level (the Church as a whole). Let it begin with you.

2. Live at a higher standard.

After enduring an arduous process of approval, ambassadors are given the full authority of their government to function in their place of assignment. In other words, when people look at you, they do not see you, they see Heaven. God has entrusted us with the authority to represent Heaven on Earth.

This means that when you are the grocery store, Heaven is with you. When you move into a new neighborhood, Heaven has moved in. When you are pumping your gas, Heaven is there. When you go into your job on Monday, Heaven is coming with you. In every area of life when faced with a predicament, we must ask ourselves: how would my King and the people of Heaven respond?

Ambassadors also do not visit places where they should not be seen nor do things that would bring shame to their country. Due to their powers of representation, they live at a higher standard than the common citizen. Paul says it best when he wrote to the Ephesians,

> "I therefore, a prisoner for the Lord, urge you to walk in a manner *worthy* of the calling to which you have been called."
> (Ephesians 4:1)

3. Seek to expand His influence.

Earthly kings in every kingdom desired to increase the influence of their reign. It is not an evil desire.

The desire itself is amoral; it is the person that possesses the desire which causes it to be good or evil. In essence, it is what they do with it that makes good or bad. As a greedy, stubborn, and arrogant king engages this desire of the heart, it manifests itself in dictatorial control and conquest. As a benevolent king engages this desire, it manifests itself in freedom and liberation for others.

Jesus, being the greatest King of all, carries within His heart to spread the influence of His reign in order to set the captives free and lighten the load of the heavy-burdened. He knows that when people are under the rule of the kingdom of darkness, then pain, slavery, bitterness, and destruction become commonplace. Our King is not satisfied until He sees His Kingdom spread into every part of the world (Matt. 13:33).

The way He gets His word out is through His messengers. This is why we as ambassadors need to seek to expand His influence every day. If we do not speak, then the message will not be heard (Rom. 10:14-17).

Choosing to not live this way will leave us in the same rut modern-day Christianity created for us. We will continue living disillusioned and empty lives void of God's supernatural touch.

4. Stay in constant communication.

As we seek to live out our assignment on Earth, there is one practice we must consistently maintain in order for us to be successful ambassadors for the Kingdom – stay in constant communication with our homeland. Since we do not possess any landlines to phone Home, God has sealed the Holy Spirit inside of us.

To show our allegiance to our King, we surrendered our lives to the Governor, the Holy Spirit. He governs our daily lives and supplies us with our instructions for the day.

Those who are truly surrendered will experience random detours and impromptu nudges on their hearts to divert from their regularly scheduled calendar to impact someone's life.

What is beautiful about being close to the Holy Spirit is that the more time we spend communing with Him, the more we begin to look like our King. We are deeply transformed from the inside-out and when people look at us, they will not see a difference between our heart and His heart.

Spend time with the Holy Spirit. He is a Person, not a thing. He has a will (Acts 13:2) and emotions (Eph. 4:30). Speak with Him. He has plans for your life and wants to use you, no matter your upbringing, personality, race, and any other excuse we try to give Him to discredit ourselves.

*   *   *   *   *

It was my turn to place the more expensive New York Strip steaks, zucchini, and asparagus on the grocery conveyor belt.

"How is your day going?"

The clerk assisting me with the transaction asked me this question as I'm seething internally. Mustering up all of the joy that remained, I responded with a simple,

"Great. It's so beautiful outside."

Living in Florida means it is beautiful outside almost every day because of near-perfect weather. Even though it seemed like my response was not common, it was essentially a cop-out answer for me.

It is a routine response in my eyes because I use it to freshen up conversations, simultaneously seeking to avoid engagement. In a few moments, however, my subsequent experience would not be so routine.

"And your total is $34.67"

Seeing those numbers on the checkout screen caused a bit of bewilderment. I began calculating the cost again as if the clerk and the system got it completely wrong. I crunched the numbers and added the sales tax, but it did not seem to add up.

As I turned my attention from my phone to the actual checkout screen, I witnessed the reason why the price fell under the $35 God instructed me to give. The sales tax totaled to $0. As in, nothing, zilch, nil, nada (for my Spanish friends).

Before they could change anything, I paid for the food and headed to my car completely in awe. And again, I heard God whisper to my heart.

"Christian, whose money is it?"
"Yours, Lord. It's all Yours."
"And I know how to handle My money, don't I?"
"Yes, Lord, You do."
"Trust Me next time. If I say it'll cost $35, then I'll make sure it does."

And with the closing of our conversation, I took the food to our friends' place where we enjoyed a beautiful dinner.

As we are laughing away at the table, inwardly my heart is opening up to the power of spreading His Kingdom and realizing that as I do it, I don't have to be affected by the systems that govern the Earth. I no longer had to worry about provision because I knew that as long as I focus on expanding His influence unto the world, the King will expand His resources unto me.

Embrace the ambassador within.

6

Live as Sons and Daughters of the King

 You are royalty. God doesn't come through for you based on your performance, but your position.

"Are you serious? Please don't tell me you've lost your birth certificate."

Judging by the tone of Chantal's voice, I can tell she was not happy. In fact, she happened to be quite livid. My wife is Australian, which means we had to jump through several hoops and complete a book's worth of paperwork to finalize her immigration process to the United States.

Our entire eight-month journey led up to this point, with it all being culminated with a final interview. The immigration officer would determine whether our marriage is worthy of the United States seal. Needless to say, our future in the U.S. hinged entirely on this interview.

And here we both are, frantically looking throughout every square inch of our two-bedroom apartment the night before the interview. We were searching to find the one document we needed to complete the pre-interview checklist and things were not looking good.

> "I can't believe you lost it. How are we going to show up without it?"

After thirty minutes of excavating every corner of our small apartment, the spirit of teamwork shifted to the spirit of blame.

> "Stop blaming me. You've had the paper confirming our interview for six weeks and you ask me *tonight* about my birth certificate?"

On the night before Chantal and I had to prove our love, our love was truly being tested. By the end of the night, we both went to sleep praying with all our hearts for God to come through the next day because we surely needed a miracle.

> "God told me you both are going to have favor with the man who's going to interview you."

Just as we were parking our car at the interview office and getting our paperwork ready the next day, Chantal receives a text from someone who knew today was our final interview. This meant a lot to us because we decided to show up anyway and stick together as a team.

We knew Satan wanted to tear us apart and we weren't going to let him win. We also showed up because we didn't want to rob God of an opportunity to produce a miracle. Chantal shared this text with me as we took our number and waited for our names to be called. I felt a sense of peace over us, even though I objectively knew we still lacked an important document that could cause us to get rejected indefinitely!

"Christian and Chantal Santiago."

After what seemed like an eternity, we heard our names. We then stood up and headed towards the agent who called us.

*   *   *   *   *

If you've lived on this Earth long enough, there's no doubt you have heard of the Greek god Zeus at some point. If you have heard about Zeus, then surely you have heard about his son, Hercules. What catches my attention about their relationship with one another are not the mythical pictures they present, but the ideology many of us believe to be true – mainly as it pertains to the power of family traits.

Your Royal Position

With Hercules being the son of Zeus, many of us would instinctively believe he would be somewhat supernatural. He would not be an ordinary child.

It would be tough to believe Zeus would have a son who would be rendered powerless. If Hercules were, in fact, ordinary and possessed no powers, it would present a confusing picture to many because we know families pass down traits to one another. This perfectly summed up my friend's first encounter with my father during my freshman year of college. She turned to me with a giant grin spread across her face, and uttered the words, "Everything makes so much sense now, Christian. Now I see why you're so crazy."

If it is natural for us to believe traits can be passed down the family lineage, then ask yourself this question: If God Almighty were to have children, what would they be like? If Hercules is powerful like his father Zeus, then what words would be used to describe God's children? Would words like powerful, strong, and secure or ones like weak, powerless and insecure characterize the sons and daughters of God Almighty?

An outsider can easily peer inside our world and take a few moments to definitely declare that words like weak, powerless, and insecure describe the children of God more than words like powerful, strong, and secure.

The first set of words were meant to be our destiny, but we have allowed the second set of words to be our reality.

Through our submission, the enemy of our souls has crafted a world where the Church is just as worried as the world. We have permitted him to create a place where the children of God are just as insecure as those who have not become His children yet (John 1:12, 1 John 3:9-10). I'm not espousing an "us vs. them" mentality, as I wholeheartedly believe in unifying every person under Christ regardless of their background and current situation. What I am espousing is that there should be a clear distinction between the believer and non-believer.

Just as there's a distinct difference between darkness and light, oil and water, so there should be a clear distinction with how a Citizen of Heaven operates and thinks compared to a Citizen of Earth. But, sadly, this is not the reality of our world. There must be a cure to this epidemic, for God does not leave us defenseless and powerless.

There is a truth we must embrace if we are going to be set free and stay free (John 8:31-32). This truth is simply this – fully accepting our position as royalty.

Peasants or Princes/Princesses?

How do you see yourself? What words would *you* use to describe yourself? I know one word I would use to describe you if you have said 'yes' to following Jesus – royalty. What is beautiful to know is that God sees you the same way! He views you in the light of royalty as opposed to the darkness of normalcy.

Unfortunately, because of the false humility-infested church atmosphere and our self-promotion culture, it is tough to declare yourself as royalty without being seen as someone who is enveloped with themselves or being overly puffed up from either side – even if both of these are the farthest thing from the truth. Because we live in such an insecure world, being secure means standing out like a foreigner and being labeled disingenuous, inauthentic, and arrogant. This backlash encourages many Citizens of Heaven to live in the shadows and refrain from accepting their royal position.

My prayer for you is that you won't be defined by the opinions of others and instead be defined by the thoughts of God. You are royalty. You are a king or queen who serves under the King of kings. You have a royal position given to you paid for by the blood of Jesus (1 Peter 2:9-10). It's time to embrace our royal position as the sons and daughters of the Most High God. You do not need to apologize for it.

You can freely expect God to come through for you, dream the greatest dreams, get excited when things get tough, live to a higher standard, and stop competing with the person next to you. Royalty lives differently than the rest. Many times, we settle for being a peasant in the field instead of being a prince or princess in the palace.

For us to successfully make the transfer from the field to the palace will require a mindset shift. We cannot hope to live like royalty in our external world if our internal world does not match up. Our identity always comes before our activity.

We need a transformation of the mind if we are going to accept this gift from God (Rom. 12:1-2). I've included a prayer in the back (Appendix) to help you on your journey towards accepting your royal position. After all, the blood of Jesus flows through your veins.

*   *   *   *   *

"You both are going to have favor with the man who's going to interview you."

Those words rang inside my head as our names were called. As we greeted the agent, we followed him to his office. On the short walk there, Chantal and I shot a quick glance at one another both saying the same thing – "at least it's a man".

If the person interviewing us happened to be a woman, then we knew the prophetic word we received would be false. At least one part of it was coming true. After our glance, we smiled at each other and stepped into his office.

The agent began the interview by asking our story on how we met. We did not hold back and shared every detail, from meeting on a mission trip to me flying to Australia four months to "talk" to Chantal's parents. We were passionately sharing our story when a sudden shift occurred.

> "Now, let's look at the documents we have for your application."

As he sifted through our documents, I looked at Chantal with a giant smile just to masquerade my nervousness and calm the tension I knew she was feeling internally. Without our physical birth certificate, we truly were relying completely on our Father to come through for us.

> "I have your application filled out along with all of the required documents, including both of your birth certificates."

As he said this, my jaw dropped to the floor, even though I tried to maintain my composure. They could have carried me out of that room limp at this point.

I did not think they would use the documents we submitted nearly a year prior, especially since we were required to bring these documents physically to every previous immigration interview.

By the end of our meeting, the agent walked us to the door, turned to us and said,

> "Thank you both for what you do. We need more people like you in the world."

With this final statement, our interview was complete and the immigration journey we embarked on nearly a year prior was finally coming to a close. We truly received favor from the man who interviewed us. Our Heavenly Father came through for us in a miraculous way. The funny thing about our Father is that He doesn't just like to show up, He also likes to show off. Two hours after this miraculous turnaround, He would show us precisely how much He likes to show off.

*   *   *   *   *

Being called to a position of royalty is an honor none of us deserve. It isn't based on our merits, accomplishments, family heritage, physical appearances, cognitive abilities, etc. It is solely based on the finished work of Jesus. If Jesus did not die and resurrect, we would still be living in our old identities, unable to obtain citizenship from Heaven. We would be subject to the tyranny of Satan and permanently enslaved to our sinful nature.

Now that we are wholly liberated from their grip, we can live as the sons and daughters of God Almighty. We no longer have to live in the shadows and can step out into the forefront of society to shine. We can take our place as catalysts that bring Heaven wherever we go simply because we are secure in our royal identity and position.

Living Like Royalty

Those in positions of royalty live in a distinct way. One can tell someone is of a prestigious family by the way they operate and carry themselves. They do not live or think like ordinary people.

Since we belong to the most prestigious family under the name of Christ, we must live differently. Things must change in our mindsets and how we live in the outside world. Luckily, there are three simple ways we can do that.

1. Develop an abundance mentality.

If someone chooses to forsake everything to follow Jesus and becomes a "new creation", one of the areas that must undergo a transformation is in the place of their mind.

A child of God cannot conduct their lives with the same old mindsets. One of the shifts that must take place is one from a poverty mindset to an abundance one. Living with a poverty mindset will hinder your ability to believe God to do the impossible, squelch your desire to pray for things of great magnitude, and crush your outlook on the circumstances of life. It will justify personal suffering and destroy the faith to steward dreams bigger than yourself.

People of royalty do not suffer from this mindset. They know when they eat at their father's table – the king – they can ask for whatever in his presence and not feel bad about it. They are keenly aware of their privilege that they ask for an unlimited amount of servings of the finest food and never need to apologize for it.

They do not eat the crumbs from the king but enjoy the exact delicacies offered to him. We as children of God should not feel ashamed to come to His throne with confidence and boldness to ask for things on our hearts, especially if they have been changed to reflect His heart (Heb. 4:16, Eph. 3:12).

Here's something we do not hear often in our churches – God *wants* to give you the greatest gifts. Since He is a good Father and a good King, He *wants* to bless His children lavishly. Look at what the Apostle Paul writes in the book of Romans,

> "He who did not spare his own Son but gave him up for us all, how will he not also with him graciously give us *all things*?" (Romans 8:32)

God desires to give us all things, we just need faith big enough to ask and obtain the abundance mentality to receive it without shame or guilt. When He gives to us, we should never feel bad regardless of what others say. He wants to bless us and not add any sorrow to it (Prov. 10:22).

Stop feeling bad for asking about something great. Believe Him at His word. He is for you. Now it's time you start to be for yourself. Don't think poverty, believe for abundance. When you do that, you'll stop limiting God and, in turn, stop limiting others and yourself.

2. Stop trying to prove yourself.

Being the middle child with an older brother, I wholly understand the term "sibling rivalry". For us, this term did not begin to take shape until I transitioned into my teenage years. There suddenly became a tension between us about who would get picked first for sports teams, friends, and girls (yes that area caused tension, too).

Sibling rivalry is any form creates division between the family and fosters an environment where competition is valued over collaboration. Unfortunately, it was not just existent in my home growing up, but it's also present in our churches today. There is sibling rivalry everywhere we turn. People are jealous of other's successes and quietly cheering their failures. As royalty, this should not be so.

Since in the eyes of our Father we are all royalty, trying to outdo one another in accomplishments and seeking to prove ourselves must die. We should instead devote ourselves to outdoing one another in giving honor (Rom. 12:10).

This means that people of royalty are not trying to prove their importance but are trying to uplift their siblings and glorify the Father. The Father approves of you. You don't need to be faithful for five years or give up all of your possessions to receive His approval. You already have it in its fullness. Live as though you have nothing to prove because you essentially don't.

3. Hear the Father's heartbeat.

There's something about the closeness between a father and a daughter. They have a deep connection to each other words cannot simply express. Chantal recently told me about how she lived on her father's lap throughout her childhood. She would spend countless hours sitting near him to hear his heartbeat and to stay close to him.

She is extremely close to both of her parents, but there is something about the weight of what Dad speaks that impacts her deeply. He doesn't say much, but when he does, it pierces her internally.

For some of us who have not grown up in this kind of environment or experienced this type of relationship with our father, it may be tough to understand these sentiments. Regardless of your upbringing though, our Father desires the same intimacy with His sons and daughters. His heart is for His children to live on His lap rather than at a distance. He cares that we hear His heartbeat up close over hearing His commands from far away.

It is an absolute injustice for people to never experience the tangible love and presence of the Father. Here's why: Jesus *spilled actual blood* to restore the relationship. He did not die so everything could remain the same. He died so we could experience His warm embrace every moment of our lives!

The way the veil was torn directly after the death of Jesus paints this picture perfectly.

> "And Jesus cried out again with a loud voice and yielded up his spirit. And behold, the curtain of the temple was torn in two, *from top to bottom*." (Matthew 27:50-51)

Did you notice it? The veil was torn from top to bottom, not the other way around. If a human being initiated the tearing, they would begin from the bottom, especially since it happened to be over 30 feet tall. Goliath couldn't even reach the top without help. But that's not what happened.

The tearing initiated from the top-down. In other words, Man did not begin the process, God did. The purpose of the veil being torn was not so Man could finally come *in*, it was so God could finally get *out*!

The Father desired to meet us so much He destroyed the barriers separating us. He wanted to be intimately near us that He was willing to spill blood for it. Since God made the ultimate first move, it is up to us as His children of royalty to take the next step, knowing He will draw near as we walk towards Him (James 4:8).

God did not want peasants, He wanted princes and princesses. He did not want slaves or subjects, He wanted sons and daughters. Make the choice today to not live at a distance, but to live from His lap. Choose to hear His heartbeat up close over hearing His commands from far away. The entirety of our identity and everything we do flows from Him (John 15:5). They are not based on the place of Heaven, but on the person of our Father.

When you decide to develop an abundance mentality, stop trying to prove yourself, and hear the Father's heartbeat, you will no longer be a subject in the field, but a son or daughter in the palace. Royal favor will be freely yours, and Heaven shall permeate every area of your life.

* * * * *

> "Hey Christian, I heard your interview went great today."

As I read these words on my phone, I immediately put it away without responding. Here I was on my lunch break at work and I received this random message from the mother of a friend I attended high school with.

It seemed odd to me because of two reasons – one, I have not seen my friend nor his mother in years, and two, we only shared the date of our final interview with our loved ones. How could she possibly know about it? Instead of asking her outright about the message, I chose not to respond and left her on "seen". That is, until she messaged me again the next day.

> "Hey Christian, I know you're wondering why I mentioned your interview yesterday."

Rather than repeating the same mistake of reading the message and going silent, I chose to respond and dialogue with her.

What she told me began to reveal exactly why Chantal and I received immense favor with the agent who interviewed us. In the middle of the workday, her husband called her and proceeded to share about a couple he interviewed, who met on a mission trip with one of them originating from Australia. It was in that moment where she blurted out a question,

"Are you talking about Christian and Chantal?"

"How did you know? Do you know them?"

"Yes, I do! He was our son's friend in school where they were five of the only Christians in their high school."

By the end of the conversation, I am sitting down in complete shock and awe. Out of all the people in the world to interview Chantal and me, it was the father of someone I went to high school with who was a part of a Christian group that consisted of only five people.

In the midst of that time spent together, I only met his mother but never got around to meeting his father because he worked long hours.

The odds of being interviewed by someone with this kind of connection is astronomically low – it almost fits the description of a miracle (you can be the judge of that). An extra addition to this story includes Chantal obtaining her green card in six days, as opposed to the thirty days we were instructed about. If this isn't royal favor, then I do not know what is.

Relaying this exchange to my wife brought about tears of gratitude, and prayers of thanksgiving to our Father for truly fulfilling His word. At that moment, we began to walk a little taller and began to believe for greater things because we knew we were a part of a family where the Father loves to come through His children in tangible ways.

Live as Sons and Daughters of the King.

Conclusion

All I want is the Kingdom. In the discovery of this gospel our Lord Jesus preached, I realized that this is what my soul had been desperately searching for. It truly is power for today, and hope for tomorrow. The gospel of the Kingdom is what healed my depression, poverty mindset, insecurity, false humility, and spiritual complacency. It has given me a fresh fire inside of my bones, and a greater faith inside of my mind.

All you need is the Kingdom. It is what your heart has been searching for this entire time. Contemporary Christianity has left us both empty, hopeless, and powerless. It reduced the power of Christ to just a two-hour meeting on a specific day of the week.

Even as these two-hour meetings unfold, every aspect of it is pristinely planned that it does not require Heaven to invade in order for the people present to be affected. People then leave the building with the same addictions, marital problems, and mental health issues. Religion kills.

The Kingdom, however, is expanding everywhere and isn't limited to a building or a block of time. Our hearts now can see Heaven manifest in our daily lives wherever we step. We can embrace our citizenship and live with purpose for the sake of our King.

We no longer need to focus on holding out for Heaven and can now live from Heaven. We can confidently declare every morning that we are new, not just better. And as we carry on with the life we have been gifted, we will seek to expand His influence, as a great Ambassador does.

We will think and operate like royalty, no longer apologizing for possessing high standards and expectations. In turn, we will experience the unexpected, yet supernatural provision, opportunities, and favor simply because we are children of God Almighty.

And most of all, we will finally be able to become who Jesus really wanted us to become all along – a Citizen, not a Christian. The days of getting His original mission, message, and focus lost in translation are over.

It's time to raise the banner of His Kingdom to the world for all to see His light and glorify our Father in Heaven (Matt. 5:16).

Go and bring Heaven to Earth.

"Your kingdom come, your will be done, *on earth as it is in heaven.*" (Matthew 6:10)

Appendix: Prayer of Royalty

In order for our mindset to be transformed into thinking and believing like royalty, we must shape our thoughts. One of the greatest ways we can shape them is through the power of words and there is no better way to use words than to pray.

Before we make the decision to pray this prayer, we must first acknowledge who we are. If we express prayers that do not go along with what we actually believe about ourselves, then we are feeding deeper into our unbelief. This is something neurologists call Cognitive Dissonance.

You are royalty. You are worthy of God's full attention. He wants to come through for you. It's not an obligation for Him to do that. Believe these truths before moving forward with the prayer, even if it takes you days or weeks to accomplish it.

Now, let's invite God to meet us and help us change our mindset together.

Father, I thank You for making me royalty. I did not deserve to be chosen, but now that I am, I will move forward with my head held high, believing for greater dreams. I will no longer apologize for expecting Your favor to be on my life. I will not fall into comparison with my brothers and sisters knowing full well that you have an infinite amount of blessings for all of Your children. I will no longer live with a poverty mindset and settle for anything less than Your best.

Now that I am a child of the Creator of the Universe, I am powerful, secure, and worthy. I can now pray specific prayers, come to Your table to ask for great things without feeling bad about it, and dream dreams that require Your full attention. Thank You for making me Your child and making me royalty.

I devote my life to helping my other brothers and sisters discover their royal identity. In the name of Jesus, I pray this prayer of royalty, Amen.

Welcome to the Royal Family of Heaven! Walk forward in your royal identity without indulging in the feeling to apologize for it. Encourage all of the others who are in the Family of God about who they are in Christ. And remember this: angels *want* to aid you in what God has called you to fulfill.

I cannot wait to see all that you would accomplish simply because you embraced your true identity. If this prayer and perspective shift helps you in any way, please share your testimony with me at **cs@christiansantiago.space**. I am praying for you always.

Acknowledgments

I would like to acknowledge, first and foremost, my wife, Chantal. She is always in my corner and asks the question, "Why not?" when I have crazy ideas about books, businesses, sermon illustrations and anything else that comes to mind.

This book is one of those crazy ideas. The gospel of the Kingdom hit me like a ton of bricks, and I couldn't help but speak to everyone about it. She encouraged me to just write a book about it.

I would also like to acknowledge my personal editor, Pamela Vasquez. Without your direct concerns and often frustrating questions, I would not have been able to communicate clearly what God has placed on my heart. I cannot wait for us to partner together on more books. Glad we're on the same team.

And lastly, I would like to acknowledge my mother-in-law, Janelle. With you being a teacher for decades, your phrase rings in my mind every time I write: "You must read over your material twice. You proofread for mistakes and then edit for improvement." My writing is infinitely better because of your wisdom.

About The Author

Christian Santiago is a native of Orlando, Florida and holds a bachelor's degree in Church Ministries from Southeastern University. He has held several positions in adult ministries, youth ministries, and children's ministries.

He is impassioned with equipping Christians to impact the culture in the 21st Century and helping people discover the original message of Jesus - which is all about the Kingdom of God.

His wife, Chantal Santiago, is from Australia and they met in the Dominican Republic on a 1Nation1Day mission trip in 2015. They married in April the following year and currently reside in Southern California where they both serve as Children's Pastors for Influence Church.

If you'd like to reach Christian to share your personal thoughts, a review of this book, prayer requests, or a desire to bring him to speak to your church, leadership team, or conference, you can email him at **cs@christiansantiago.space**.

www.ingramcontent.com/pod-product-compliance
Lightning Source LLC
Chambersburg PA
CBHW020418080526
44584CB00014B/1392